T0165007

When a
Woman
Finds
Her Moment

For the Woman in Waiting

Lisa J. Davis

WestBow
PRESS
A DIVISION OF THOMAS NELSON

Copyright © 2012 Lisa J. Davis

All rights reserved. No part of this book may be used or reproduced by any means, graphic, electronic, or mechanical, including photocopying, recording, taping or by any information storage retrieval system without the written permission of the publisher except in the case of brief quotations embodied in critical articles and reviews.

Scripture quotations noted KJV are from the King James Version of the Bible.

Scripture quotations noted NIV are from the Holy Bible, New International Version®. Copyright © 1973, 1978, 1984 Biblica. Used by permission of Zondervan. All rights reserved.

WestBow Press books may be ordered through booksellers or by contacting:

WestBow Press
A Division of Thomas Nelson
1663 Liberty Drive
Bloomington, IN 47403
www.westbowpress.com
1-(866) 928-1240

Because of the dynamic nature of the Internet, any web addresses or links contained in this book may have changed since publication and may no longer be valid. The views expressed in this work are solely those of the author and do not necessarily reflect the views of the publisher, and the publisher hereby disclaims any responsibility for them.

Any people depicted in stock imagery provided by Thinkstock are models, and such images are being used for illustrative purposes only.

Certain stock imagery © Thinkstock.

ISBN: 978-1-4497-3702-3 (sc)
ISBN: 978-1-4497-3703-0 (hc)
ISBN: 978-1-4497-3701-6 (e)

Library of Congress Control Number: 2012900960

Printed in the United States of America

WestBow Press rev. date: 01/25/2012

To my husband and our daughters, who have, through the ups and downs of life, propelled me into the place of finding my moment. To my sister and brother, who have loved me through tragedies and been a continuous place of unconditional love,

I love you dearly.

Contents

Acknowledgements

There are many friends, family, and wonderful women whom I long to meet someday who were readers on the earlier drafts of this book. Their comments and feedback have been invaluable in helping me to produce an even more professional and touching book for you.

I want to especially thank my friend Nina who challenged me to write with more clarity and tidy up the manuscripts grammar to reach a broader readership. Your honesty has helped me to produce a much better piece.

I would like to thank the line editing staff members of Westbow Press. Their expertise cannot be overlooked. The manuscript you hold in your hands is much different because of their insightful comments, suggestions, and questions.

Finally, and foremost, I would like to thank God for pouring out His love in my heart and then allowing me to share this love with you.

Introduction

And the woman was healed from that moment.
Matthew 9:22b (NIV)

I was a mess when God found me; I dare not say when I found God. I wasn't even looking for Him, which is telling of the mental and emotional mess I was in. I wanted to be loved, but I found love in the all the wrong places. I wanted to know my purpose, but I didn't have a clue what my gifts were or if I even had any. I wanted to be popular; all of my security was tied up in my being a part of the "in crowd."

Having grown up in church, you would have thought I knew better. But I didn't get it. In my thinking, God was for Sunday. All of the other days were up to me. It was that line of thinking that got me into every mess I was living in.

The significant event that started my journey toward finding my moment happened on New Year's night, 1995. I went to a Christian youth conference. I wish I could tell you I was there for good reasons, but I wasn't. My original plan was to sneak away with my boyfriend and return the final day of the conference to catch a ride back to the college dorm. However, he never showed, and my brokenheartedness led me to the best decision I have ever made. That's right, broken hearts can actually turn out well. Because my plans failed, I was in need of something to do, so I attended the conference.

I had never experienced being around young people who really wanted to live for God. I was used to playing, sleeping, and flirting in the back rows on most Sundays. This was different; it was what I had been missing.

I knew at the moment of my decision to attend the conference New Year's Day that God had a better plan for my life. I'd never raised my hand during the altar call on the outside, but in my heart, a change had occurred. I didn't doubt my salvation. I was, however, in *big* doubts about my lifestyle. I was not living for God, and it became very clear that night that I needed to learn how.

For this reason, I began a process of change like that of a caterpillar into a butterfly. I changed my television choices, the way I dressed became more conservative, and my church attendance became serious. I had long before chosen Him as Savior; it was time to make Him Lord. I had been saved from hell; now I needed saving from myself and life as I'd known it. The woman in this study needed God in much the same way.

She was a woman in waiting—but her time had come.

Envision a woman in the midst of a crowd, tears streaming down her face as she recognizes this opportunity is her chance to be healed.

It's now or never.

Until this moment, her circumstances have prohibited her from making personal contact with another human being, but she knows He is different. The force of faith urges her to press through to Him, although she weighs the consequences of being caught.

Her hair is tussled upon her head. Beads of perspiration run down her cheeks. She presses closer and closer, until finally, she forces her hand between the knees of the people in front of her and catches a piece of His robe. Tingling inside from the excitement of reaching her goal, the woman barely realizes the sudden stillness of the crowd as Jesus stops to ask, "Who touched Me?" No one else knows.

When she hears the question, she is the only one who begins to tremble. Her hands grip the seam of her own garment as she decides whether she will go to Him or run away. In this moment of decision, she looks up to see His eyes gazing at her from beyond the short distance. She gathers herself, moves toward Him, and falls down at His feet. With a racing heart and trembling lips, she struggles to explain her actions. All of the onlookers listen attentively as she recounts how she had come with an issue of blood and sought to touch His garment for a chance to be healed.

Still weeping from the intensity of the moment, she looks up at Jesus as He speaks to her. Had she heard Him right? Did He say "daughter"? Her fears begin to fade away as He speaks. His words are comforting and peaceful. Wiping her face, He lifts her to her feet. She knows all is well. She smiles to say *thank You* as she turns to leave (Mt. 9:20–22; Mark 5:24–34; Luke 8:43–48).

Can you imagine what she must have been feeling in that moment? Everything else she'd tried had failed. For the first time in twelve years, there was wholeness and peace. This was not a temporary form of relief but a lifetime cure. Her days would be changed forever.

What was it that brought about this needed miracle? Jesus Himself said, "Daughter, *your faith* has healed you" (emphasis added) (Mark 5:34a). She had a willingness to believe that Jesus would make a difference in her life. Despite the failures of all else in her past, she did not consider giving up to be an option.

How about you, dear one? Have you found yourself in a mess? This study is the perfect opportunity to get up and dust off your faith. Are you ready to *believe* that Jesus is able to bring healing to your situation? Do you *trust* that Jesus is willing to give you a new beginning full of peace? While you may not be able to confidently respond to these questions at this point, it is my purpose to aid you in getting to a firm yes by the end of this study.

This woman with the issue of blood had to be convinced of two things if the circumstances were going to change: Jesus was *able* to heal her, and Jesus was *willing* to restore (Jer. 32:27; Mark 1:41). There were many other people who touched Jesus that day, but her touch was unlike the others'. The force of her faith got His attention (and a place in the Holy Scriptures). It was her moment to be healed.

After years of suffering and discouragement, how was she able to hope for any change? What caused her to believe that

Jesus was unlike anything she'd already tried? I believe this biblical biography holds the answers we desire.

Throughout this study, space is provided for recording personal time with God. There are four sections: "My Special Moments," "Prayer," "Going Deeper," and, "Faith Confessions." "My Special Moments" are for quiet times of reflection. Use the journaling space to write down points of interest or life examples that personally connect you with the chapter.

"Prayer" is a special way for you to communicate with God using related points from the lesson. There is space provided for personalizing your prayer using the reflections written in "My Special Moments."

"Going Deeper" provides a devotional thought for meditation throughout the day. This is followed by "Faith Confessions," which gives you scriptural promises to declare over your life.

My prayer for you as we journey in the midst of this crowd is that these life principles will encourage you to believe Jesus for permanent peace and freedom in your life. I have prayed for you, dear one, and I believe that this will truly be your season.

Congratulations

You have found your moment to be healed!

Life Principle 1

God Has Time for Me

Mark 5:24
So Jesus went with him.

The woman approached Jesus while He was on His way to help Jairus's critically ill daughter. Jairus had persuaded Jesus to come to his home and lay hands on the child so that she would live. Jesus had agreed and was walking with Jairus when He was stopped by the woman's touch.

Jesus could have come back after attending to Jairus's daughter to heal the woman. A few more days or hours probably would not have mattered much for her, but time was running out for the young child. In spite of this, Jesus stopped for the woman the moment she touched Him.

What an amazing aspect of this woman's encounter with Jesus! He took time to stop for her. He was not bound by the pressing need of the moment. He was not fearful that in stopping to help her He might not reach the sick girl in time.

Jesus cares about each person's situation. He is never too busy to meet the need of a hurting individual. You can rest assured that He is equally concerned about your situation. He cares so much about you that He will stop along *His* way and meet *your* needs.

My Special Moments

Reflect on His willingness to care for your concerns. Write down exactly how you feel and what you would like God to take time to do for you. The list can be as long or as short as you wish. After you write down your thoughts, take time to pray aloud to God.

_____

_____

_____

_____

_____

_____

_____

_____

_____

_____

_____

_____

Prayer

Dear Father, You are so amazing. You take time just for me. You are not too busy for my family, my work, or my life. You care enough for me to help me. Help me to have the touch of this woman. I want to touch You in a way that causes Your power to work in my life. Thank You for taking time for (pray about the thoughts you wrote down). In Jesus' Name, I believe that Your power will bring lasting changes. Amen.

Going Deeper

Jesus went with Jairus. Jesus stopped for the woman. He had time for them both. The original word used here for "Jesus went with him" is *aperchomai,* meaning to go away in order to follow any one. In Matthew 9:19, the word used is *akoloutheo,* meaning to accompany him. Jesus is willing to follow us and accompany us in our times of difficulty. This is huge. Usually, the more difficult a situation may be, the less we find another person willing to be with us through it.

In seasons like this, certain questions come to mind:

> "If God loves me, why would this happen?"
> "If God is love, how could this go on so long?"
> "If I want to be healed and God wants me to be healed, what is going on?"

While I am not sure if we can really understand the dynamics of this, I recall one minister who was given this response: "Trust requires unanswered questions." That answer may or may not ease our concerns, but there is a silver lining to all of this:

God does care and He is in control.

Here's what we can find from the Bible about how God sees these moments:

1 Peter 4:12 Dear friends, do not be surprised at the fiery ordeal that has come on you to test you, as though something strange were happening to you.

Ephesians 6: 16 In addition to all this, take up the shield of faith, with which you can extinguish all the flaming arrows of the evil one.

John 16:33 "I have told you these things, so that in me you may have peace. In this world you will have trouble. But take heart! I have overcome the world."

Romans 8:31 What, then, shall we say in response to these things? If God is for us, who can be against us?

Of course, some may be able to say a parent was there for them or a close friend. Only those who love us the deepest are willing to be with us in our greatest times of need. Jesus is *always* among those who dare hold our hands in these moments. Those who help us give what they can and even sometimes sacrifice their time, abilities, and resources. And so it is with Christ. With the sacrifice of His life at the cross, He made available the peace, joy, and strength we need to pull through any situation.

Faith Confessions
GOD HAS TIME FOR ME

God has thoughts of peace for me.
Jeremiah 29:11

When I call upon God, He hears me.
Jeremiah 33:3

The Lord delivers me from all my fears.
Psalm 34:4

I draw near to God and He draws near to me.
James 4:8

Because I seek God, He rewards me.
Hebrews 11:6

Life Principle 2

The God of the Multitudes Is Also the God of Individuals

Mark 5:24
... a large crowd followed ...

The woman had a hint that despite the large congregation of people, she would have a chance to get her personal need ministered to. She was not intimidated by the size of the group. She did not feel apprehensive about being among so many others. She was drawn to this God of the multitudes, because somehow, she knew He was also the God of individuals.

Jesus had a charisma about His lifestyle that drew large groups of people to Him. He was usually teaching before a crowd, feeding the masses, or healing in the midst of an assembly. His life was characterized by ministering to the multitudes. He had to purposely go off to a mountain just to pray and spend time alone with the Father.

Although Jesus was always concerned about the multitudes, He proved over and over again to be the God of individual. Among crowds of people, He found ways to minister to specific individuals—the man who was born blind (John 9), the woman who lived bent over (Luke 13), the paralytic (Mt. 9), just to name a few. This woman in our text understood God's heart for the individual person within the crowd.

It is a wonderful feeling to know that when you stand in front of crowded altars on a Sunday morning or during a midweek service that God hears each individual prayer. The hearts that come before His throne are singled out for the angels, in God's will, to bring answers to each personal need and desire.

My Special Moments

Reflect on His Father's heart for you as His child. Jot down how you feel about God's love for you as a specific woman. The list can be as long or as short as you wish. After you write down your thoughts, take time to pray aloud to God.

_____

_____

_____

_____

_____

_____

_____

_____

_____

_____

_____

_____

_____

_____

_____

Prayer

Dear Father, Your love is incredible. When You look upon the earth, You see me. You are able to pick out my voice and my heart's cry from among all the prayers that come before You. You are so unlimited in Your ability to meet the needs of others and mine at the same time. Help me to trust Your love that You have allotted just for me. Thank You for proving my value to You (pray about the thoughts you wrote down). In Jesus' Name, thank You for giving me worth and significance. Amen.

Going Deeper

Jesus understood what it was like to feel pressed on all sides. The Bible gives four distinct words in the original texts to describe this: *synthlibo, sympnigo, synecho,* and *apothlibo.* By definition, these words encompass the meanings: to press on all sides; to choke utterly; to press round or throng one so as almost to suffocate; to press on every side; to squeeze, press hard; of pressing out grapes and olives. It was this understanding that helped him relate so intimately with the woman. She knew all too well what it was to feel pressed.

She was pressed on every side by physical, mental, emotional, financial, and relational pressures. I can imagine she felt that her life was suffocating what little strength and zeal she had left. If she could have worn a motto on her T-shirt, it would have said, "I'm sick and tired of being sick and tired."

Having faith like this takes courage. Jeremiah 32:27 states, "I am the LORD, the God of all mankind. Is anything too hard for me?" The Greek word for "anything" is *dabar,* meaning "words, business, occupation, matter, case." The word for "too hard" is *pala,* meaning "beyond one's power" or "too difficult to do or understand." Her trust was a living witness that she believed there was not any matter in her life that was beyond His power or understanding. In spite of all the pressure she was under, she chose to believe. This is courageous.

Most of us probably identify more readily with the man in Mark 1:40–41. He had faith that God *could*, but he didn't have faith that God *would*.

The woman believed both. The lesson we learn from this woman is simple but very profound. When you feel pressed, the only response that can save you is to press forward. Be courageous enough to believe God can *and* God will. Her refusal to give up released the chokehold on her life. Instead of giving in to being overwhelmed, she insisted she would overcome.

Faith Confessions

THE GOD OF THE MULTITUDES IS ALSO THE GOD OF INDIVIDUALS

I may be pressed, but I am remembered by God
and I have strength for each day.
2 Corinthians 4: 8, 9

I am determined to have God's joy.
James 1:2

I will wait on the Lord and be of good courage.
He will strengthen me. He will save me.
Psalms 27:14; 20:22

Even when nothing seems to be going right,
I will rejoice in God for He is my strength.
Habakkuk 3:17–19

I will keep the faith. I will be patient.
I have an inheritance of God's promises.
Hebrews 6:12

Life Principle 3

It's Never Too Late

Mark 5:25
... for twelve years.

This woman, like so many of us, had battled with this situation for years. She had to learn to live with her infirmity. She was probably used to the jeers, whispers, and pointed fingers. Yet, the hope she had inside of her for a change would not die.

We all face challenges and obstacles in our lives that bring about dis-ease. Hers was a disease in her physical body. However, you may struggle with dis-ease in a relationship, dis-ease on a job, or dis-ease from your childhood. The causes of dis-ease are endless.

The good news of this women's testimony is that delay does not mean denial. The passage of long periods of time can be discouraging during difficult seasons of life. Because we know that she was a woman, she had to have been more than twelve years of age. There was a time in her past that she was well. She knew what it was like to be free, and she desired to have that freedom again, no matter how long it took.

There are times in life when you may happen upon a situation that causes an unforeseen disturbance in the tranquility you once knew. The sudden death of a relative, discovery about a husband's affair, a steady plunge into an addiction—these types of circumstances can bring years of suffering and undesirable consequences. But there is always hope.

The fact that the Bible records the number of years associated with this situation indicates that God is mindful of the length of time you have been dealing with your issues. God may not always deliver you right way, but

He can give you an enduring hope as you wait for His move in your life. Right in the middle of what looks hopeless; God can deliver you *in* the situation until He delivers you *from* the season. Seasons change. Keep holding on.

My Special Moments

Reflect on any lingering situations that you desire for God to heal. Write down how you feel about the peace that God makes available to you during these difficult times. The list can be as long or as short as you wish. After you write down your thoughts, take time to pray aloud to God.

_____

_____

_____

_____

_____

_____

_____

_____

_____

_____

_____

_____

Prayer

Dear Father, You are wiser than I am. There are things that happen in my life that I will never understand. Help me to believe in Your ability to give me daily strength as I wait for changes You will bring in my life. Thank You for giving me hope (pray about the thoughts you wrote down). In Jesus' Name, I believe You will heal my situation at just the right time. Amen.

Going Deeper

The cause of her blood condition is not very clear, but to the world of her time, it meant she was unclean and unfit (Lev. 15:25). The religious leaders would have been familiar with laws concerning a woman in her condition; she was to be considered an outcast (Lev. 15:26, 27, 31).

Some of the repercussions of such a label meant that she was isolated from fellowship within the place of worship, within the public places, and even included the laws forbidding her to have sexual relations with a husband (if she even had one at this point; Lev. 15:33). The only way she could have been purified or made clean would have been by correcting her condition (Lev 15:28–30).

Her healing was not just about the physical freedom she desired but also the social and relational freedoms every human being *needs*. According to Vines Expository Dictionary, the term for her situation was *aposunagogos,* meaning put out of the congregation. The opposite, *archisunagogos*, meaning a ruler of the congregation, defined Jairus.

Yet, they both stood in a place at the mercy of Jesus. Before Him, they were both in equal need. One who was rejected and one who was accepted were both in the season of hardship. Jesus came for the hurts of each of us, regardless of the life situations in which we find ourselves. In Him, there is no situation too big or insignificant for healing and restoration.

Faith Confessions

IT'S NEVER TOO LATE

I am accepted in Jesus.
Ephesians 1:6

There is not anything my life
that is too hard for God.
Jeremiah 32:27

Because I seek God first,
all my needs are met.
Matthew 6:31–33

I give my cares to God and
choose not to worry
because God cares about my life.
1 Peter 5:7

I choose to trust God completely
and will not lean on the limits
of human understanding.
Proverbs 3:5

Life Principle 4

Situations That Have Gotten Worse Can Get Better

Mark 5:26
... yet instead of getting better,
she grew worse.

By the time she found Jesus among the crowd, she was financially broke and in a more severe condition. Up to that point, she had tried everything that she could. She went to every physician she could find. She attempted every treatment. None of the surgical procedures worked. Not one of the medications proved effective.

Everything she tried medically had failed. In the process, she spent all her money searching for the cure. Despite all her efforts, she never found release from her circumstances. And when she thought it could not possibly get any worse, it did.

Surely the doctors had given her all kinds of preventions and prescriptions, but they were not able to help her. She was at the end of her natural resources. Jesus had become her only hope.

In an era when self-help has become so popular, you can understand why she spent all her time, efforts, and money trying to find a solution to her problem. She was reaching out for anything that may relieve the suffering. But while she attempted to find *a* way out, she had not yet found *the* Solution.

Jesus is *the* Solution. He can use a doctor, a medication, or a surgical procedure; but He alone is the source of healing. Everything else is resource. It is not in the instrument He chooses but in Him. She had discovered through experience that there was no hope in finding an alternate answer, but she was determined to get in contact with the Solution. Her healing came through faith, believing He was the answer.

My Special Moments

Reflect on any substitute solutions that you tried that ended in disappointment. Jot down how you feel about God Himself being the answer to the problems in life. The list can be as long or as short as you wish. After you write down your thoughts, take time to pray aloud to God.

_____

_____

_____

_____

_____

_____

_____

_____

_____

_____

_____

_____

_____

_____

_____

Prayer

Dear Father, You are irreplaceable. There is no other solution to my hurts besides You. I have tried so many things in this life, but only You satisfy. Thank You for being my hope (pray about the thoughts you wrote down). In Jesus' Name, I know You are the hope that will not fail. Amen.

Going Deeper

The word for suffered in this scripture is *paschō,* meaning to be affected or have been affected, to suffer sadly or be in a bad plight. She did not just have an unfortunate situation; she was in *very bad* circumstances. The phrase, "she had spent all," *dapanaō,* means to incur expense or to waste everything. The book of Luke defines this as, "all her living," *bios,* meaning that by which life is sustained: resources, wealth, and goods. It was not just a physical mess she was enduring; she had hardships in every area of her life.

To add insult to injury, she not only faced zero return from her expenses, but the situation over the years became *cheirōn,* meaning to get worse and worse. She had used up every resource to only be left in a continually depressed state. She literally had nothing left … except her faith.

I read a T-shirt once with these words printed in big bold letters, "When all else fails, try God." I believe if the woman in the text could rewrite the T-shirt, it would read, "Before all else fails, try God." She was in a desperate place. In that moment, Christ became her priority, and she had one goal in mind: *get to Jesus.* He was all she had left.

This is what makes her determination against the odds so inspiring. In light of what had to have been such a traumatic state of suffering and loss, it blesses me that she refused to let the circumstances steal her focus for freedom. Lord, may we continually rely on You to help us not be distracted by the negatives but to stay focused on the possibilities in God.

Faith Confessions

SITUATIONS THAT HAVE GOTTEN WORSE CAN GET BETTER

God I thank You that even what
was meant for evil,
You can bring good out of it.
Genesis 50:20

I believe God's promises for me
are victory and He overturns
all the negatives against me.
Esther 9:1

There is not anything that can
separate me
from God's love for me.
Romans 8:39

All things are possible with God.
Mark 9:23, 24

My life path is getting
brighter and brighter.

Proverbs 4:18

Life Principle 5

God Uses Others' Life Stories to Inspire Me

Mark 5:27
When she heard about Jesus ...

Someone told her about Jesus. Perhaps she heard about the time He healed the leper (Mt. 8), how He delivered a man of Capernaum from a tormenting spirit (Mark 1), or that He turned water into wine (John 2). Whatever she heard, it was enough to convince her that a real opportunity for healing had come her way.

The woman was so convinced by what she heard that she wasted no time in going to find this person who was more than a man. By His appearance, He was just another human being. He was the son of Joseph and Mary, a mere carpenter by trade. But she saw beyond His earthly apparel and accepted Him as more than a son of man.

Her conviction caused her to act on what she had heard. The woman recognized that her moment had come because of the reputation of His presence. He was the answer for which she had been searching. The woman refused to allow the obstacle of the crowd to come between her and the destiny she believed was hers.

She made a decision to get close enough to touch Him on the backside of His cloak. Although the healing would come by Jesus, she had to do her part. Her participation in the healing was to reach out her hand to Him. The condition had forbid her to have a right to even be in the crowd. But she believed by the testimonies she had heard that it was worth the costs she may face to be there. She had no money to offer for His help. All the woman had to give was her faith. And she gave all that she had by her touch.

My Special Moments

Reflect on biblical examples of God's miraculous power, testimonies that you have heard from others, and the names of God that reveal the many facets of His character. Write down what you have heard about God. The list can be as long or as short as you wish. After you write down your thoughts, take time to pray aloud to God.

_____

_____

_____

_____

_____

_____

_____

_____

_____

_____

_____

_____

_____

_____

Prayer

Dear Father, I want to know more about You. Show me places in the Bible that help me to "hear" more about You. Lead me into conversations with people that reveal Your work in the lives of people who live today. Show me how to give an expression of my faith to You. Give me courage to overcome any obstacles between us. Thank You for giving me new insight into who You are (pray about the thoughts you wrote down). In Jesus' Name, I desire to give You what I can offer. Amen.

Going Deeper

Mark says, "she heard" *akouō*. It means she understood and considered what was told to her about Him. She had just enough time to decide that if He could help someone else, He could help her. The woman acted on this, and bending low from behind, she touched the very place that represented wholeness to the culture of her time: the hem of His garment, *kraspedon,* called *tzitziyot* in Hebrew. This part of His robe represented several things to her that day.

> These *tzitziyot* were a point of contact she needed to help her release her faith to receive a miracle in her life. What did they represent? First, they represented the Word of God, which is always the place where we can find healing for all the needs in our life. Second, the fringes also represented the authority of Yeshua. She had heard that many people were healed by Yeshua, that He taught with authority and when He spoke, people were healed.
>
> Third, there was even more to these fringes. The prophet Malachi spoke of the Messiah of Israel and said of Him, *"But for you who revere My name, the sun of righteousness will rise with healing in His wings" (Mal. 4:2).* The Hebrew word for "wings" used in this passage is *kanaf,* which is a word that specifically means the fringe-like feathers

or edges of a bird's wing, not the whole wing. All of us have seen an eagle or hawk circling in the summer sky and have seen these fringe-like feathers. This word, therefore, had two meanings and could be translated wings, or fringes. The woman had heard Yeshua was the Messiah. Perhaps she remembered this messianic promise from the scroll of Malachi and thought, if I am to be healed, then will it be found in His wings ... His *tzitziyot*? By faith, she reached out and touched the fringes, and was healed. (Ressler)

It meant so much to her: the Word of God, the authority of God, and the wings of God. Wow. It means the same for us this very day (Heb. 13:8). The Word of God: "He sent His word and healed them and delivered them from their destructions" (Psalm 107:20 KJV). The authority of God: the centurion in a moment of great faith spoke of this authority when he proclaimed of Christ, "but speak the word only, and my servant shall be healed" (Mt. 8:5–13 KJV).

The wings of God: "The Lord recompense thy work, and a full reward be given thee of the Lord God of Israel, under whose wings thou art come to trust" (Ruth 2:12 KJV). These were the words Boaz used to explain to Ruth why she had come to find favor in his sight. May the Lord grant that each woman who finds this book in her hands will bear this testimony on her life, to know Jesus in this way as this beloved woman did those many years ago. After all, if He did it for her then, He can do it for you now.

Faith Confessions

GOD USES OTHERS' LIFE STORIES TO INSPIRE ME

There is no respect of persons with God.
What God did for this woman,
He can and wants to do for me.
Romans 2:11

Because I am seeking God,
He will reward me
as He did those of faith in Hebrews.
Hebrews 11:6

God healed this woman,
I know God can heal me.
Matthew 9:22

God cared when this lady was crying,
I know God cares when I cry.
Luke 7:13

God forgave this woman.
I know God can forgive me.
John 8:11

Life Principle 6

God's Truth Outweighs My Reality

Mark 5:28
... I will be healed.

What she had heard about Jesus started her to thinking. She was led to believe that even a "little" touch was enough. The woman internalized what someone shared with her. The faith of another was now *her* faith.

This confidence enabled the woman to think beyond her life circumstance and believe in the Truth of who Jesus was. Not anything in her natural thinking could have helped her come to this conclusion. In reality, she was not worthy to be there. In reality, she was forbidden to touch anyone else. In reality, she had been sick for twelve years and had gotten worse. In reality, she already tried everything she could think of and nothing had worked. But the Truth was ...

Jesus was a Healer, and she believed it! She did not just press through a crowd that day, she mentally pressed past all her realities. She did not let her natural circumstances determine what Jesus could do for her.

Her faith was so strong in His ability to heal her that she decided to touch a piece of His clothing as He walked past. Something in the woman's thoughts allowed her to understand the vastness of His power. His power was greater than her realities. His power would not allow her realities to cause her touch to be ineffective. She determined that Jesus was more than enough. He proved her to be right.

My Special Moments

Reflect on your personal thoughts concerning God's Truth as a greater force than the realities in your life. Jot down how you feel about the vast power of God. The list can be as long or as short as you wish. After you write down your thoughts, take time to pray aloud to God.

_____

_____

_____

_____

_____

_____

_____

_____

_____

_____

_____

_____

_____

_____

Prayer

Dear Father, Your Truth outweighs my reality. In reality, I am unworthy, but You consider me worthy in Christ (Eph. 1:6). In reality, I make mistakes, but You have called me the righteousness of God in Christ (Phil. 3:9). Thank You for looking past my realities (pray about the thoughts you wrote down). In Jesus' Name, I trust Your power to be effective in my life. Amen.

Going Deeper

Her thoughts opened her mouth for miracles to happen. The original word for thought here is *legō,* meaning to say and affirm over and over. It was this progression of what she heard affecting what she thought that influenced what she said over and over. She heard a testimony that got her to a place of hope. Hope opened her mouth for healing. This implies that what I hear makes a huge impact on my mind and my mouth. What have you been hearing lately? Matthew specifically calls attention to the fact she did not say the words audibly but "within herself" (Mt. 9:21).

It makes the question more appropriate then to ask, "What have you been hearing on the inside?" (Prov. 18:21). Words are containers for life or death; there is no middle ground. "I shall be whole" were words of life that rose within her over and over at that pivotal moment. They mean to save and be rescued from danger and suffering and to be restored to health, *sōzō.* If the recorder in my mind is on negative, I have the right to switch the message. Through Bible study, listening to encouraging CDs and inspirational music, or watching ministry on television, I can begin to hear a positive message.

I have to ask myself the following questions to find out my true a reality check. *Am I willing to take the risks, or am I willing to stay as I am? Am I willing to fight, or am I willing to give up? Do I believe God is willing and able or that He is not?* The only way to tell is by listening in on what's been playing on my mental recorder. If I've been meditating on negative, defeating thoughts, I have the right to replace them.

Time spent in the car can become a place for renewing my mind through purposefully turning on Christian radio or listening to sermons on topics that relate to my circumstances. I can find a quiet time early in the morning, before anyone else is up in the house, to meditate on Scriptures. Sometimes, changing my conversation, or those with whom I converse, may be necessary. Whatever it takes, I can tune out the negative and turn up hope within me.

Faith Confessions
GOD'S TRUTH OUTWEIGHS MY REALITY

God calls things that be not
as though they were in my
life and I agree with God.
Romans 4:17

Whenever God speaks, whatever He says is so.
He has spoken through the Bible
good things over my life as His daughter.
Genesis 1: 3,9; Jeremiah 29:11

God calls His divine purpose in my life
even before I am
who I will become in Him.
Judges 6:11, 12

Regardless of all life may bring,
I am still more than a conqueror
through God's love. Romans 8:37

I agree with God that in my life everything
bows at the name of Jesus.
His name brings safety to me.
Philippians 2:10; Proverbs 18:10

Life Principle 7

God's Perfect Timing Is Now

Mark 5:29
Immediately her bleeding
stopped ...

Her issue was resolved immediately. Not all of God's answers to prayer are instantaneous, but He hears each one from the first moment someone asks (Dan. 10:12). For example, Hannah prayed for God to give her a child. Hannah did not leave with the baby in her arms, but she left the temple with faith in her heart to conceive (1 Sam. 1).

God's plan for her answer was released in the instant she prayed in faith, although the benefits showed up at an appointed time later. The consistency between Hannah's answer to prayer and the woman in the crowd is that God responded to both requests immediately; it was only the timing of the manifestation that differed.

At the moment the woman touched Him, her health was restored. This time, she would not be disappointed, like all the other attempts. This time, there was a difference. She would not go home as she had come. She finally had the healing that she desired.

The change in her life was so dramatic that she could feel a change in her body. She did not have to guess if touching Jesus worked. She did not have to try and touch Him again, "just in case." She knew right then that she was completely healed of her troubles.

The affliction would not torment her body any longer. Not only was she healed of the physical attributes of her illness, she was also freed from the emotional pain of living with such a condition. She would now be able to go among the people freely. She would actually have the privilege of going inside the temple gates to worship. She would know once again what it felt like to be touched by another. Her clothing would no longer be stained and smell of dried blood. She was free.

My Special Moments

Reflect on the assurance of God's immediate response to your prayer, although the answer may come at a later time. Write down how you feel about God's response time to your prayers. The list can be as long or as short as you wish. After you write down your thoughts, take time to pray aloud to God.

_____

_____

_____

_____

_____

_____

_____

_____

_____

_____

_____

Prayer

Dear Father, You hear all of my prayers. There have been times when I felt as if You were not listening and then all of a sudden, You sent an answer better than I had hoped for. You have the ability to do wonderful things behind the scenes, and at just the right time, an answer from heaven appears. Thank You for giving me faith to believe for immediate miracles and patience to wait on Your perfect timing (pray about the thoughts you wrote down). In Jesus' Name, I believe You know when to manifest my miracle. Amen.

Going Deeper

She felt it (*ginōskō*). This kind of feeling did not just mean she had a strong feeling about it; she actually *knew* it was different this time. Every other endeavor left her hope dwindling away. I can imagine there was always a sliver of expectation yet each time she had to walk away from those experiences without the feeling that everything was changed. And now she felt the healing.

The word for healing, *iaomai,* is physical but also includes being free from sins. This is important to note, because the word for suffering here is *mastix,* defined as a misfortune sent by God to discipline or punish.

Jesus used this same word in verse 34 of this text. I believe this is very important, because it means she was not just physically freed but also forgiven.

This may very well be the most important principle in the book: to be forgiven of sin is to be blessed (Ps. 32:2; Rom. 4:8). She had only come for the physical healing, but she also received a new spiritual beginning. He healed her body, and more important, her relationship with God was restored. How many times have I gotten into a fix because of a mistake I made? I didn't just need help because of the consequences: I needed a clean slate. He gave her both.

God is good, and He does good toward His people (Ps. 73:1; 84:11). I am not saying that we can just "get away with" our sins. I do understand that He is also a loving Father who disciplines His children (Prov. 3:12). However, I am saying that God's heart never points a finger or slams the gavel. He lovingly and longingly wants repentance so that we can experience His best instead of judgment.

Perhaps this is a key reason no other physician could help. There was no other place to find physical relief as well as forgiveness for the soul.

Faith Confessions
GOD'S PERFECT TIMING IS NOW

The plan for my life will
surely come to pass
and it will not be late.
Habakkuk 2:3

The Lord is not slow
concerning His promises to me.
2 Peter 3:9

God knows how
to bring a "suddenly" into my life.
Acts 2:2

I will stand in faith and patience
because I trust
that the promises are on the way.
Hebrews 6:12

I will look to God.
I will wait for God. God will hear me.

Micah 7:7

Life Principle 8

I Have Reason to Hope When Others Do not Understand

Mark 5:30, 31
"You see the people crowding against you," his disciples answered, "and yet you can ask, 'Who touched me?'"

All of a sudden, there was stillness in the crowd. Jesus stopped in His tracks and began to look around. The disciples were dumbfounded as to why there was this sudden halt. Jairus was undoubtedly anxious as to why they were not continuing on their way to his daughter.

Surely, all the company traveling with Jesus began to whisper among themselves. "Why have we stopped?" "What is going on?" "Is everything okay?" And despite their lack of discernment for the activities of the moment, Jesus asked, "Who touched me?"

Among the hustle and bustle of this high traffic area, He was sure to be bumped and shoved, but someone had *touched* Him. He discerned the touch by the power that had gone forth out of Him (Luke 8:46). Unlike Jairus, who had placed his hope in Jesus touching his daughter, this woman had placed her hope in her ability to touch Jesus.

Of all the people who brushed against Him in the crowd, only her touch was recognized. Her presence had gone unnoticed among the crowd, but Jesus felt her touch. Only two members in the crowd were aware of the power of God that proceeded from Jesus to change a life. She felt it in her body, and Jesus acknowledged this with His words.

My Special Moments

Reflect on God's awareness of your circumstances, even when others do not understand. Jot down how you feel about God's recognition of a faith-filled touch. The list can be as long or as short as you wish. After you write down your thoughts, take time to pray aloud to God.

_____

_____

_____

_____

_____

_____

_____

_____

_____

_____

_____

_____

_____

_____

_____

Prayer

Dear Father, You are wiser than I am. There are things that happen in my life that I will never understand. Help me to believe in Your ability to give me daily strength as I wait for the changes You will bring in my life. Thank You for giving me hope (pray about the thoughts you wrote down). In Jesus' Name, I believe You will heal my situation at just the right time. Amen.

Going Deeper

We, like the woman, are partners with God. She had done her part, now it was time for Jesus to do His.

He was so full of power that she was able to touch Him so that what was in Him is what came into her life. The word here for power is *dynamis*. This word looks and sounds like the word "dynamite." An explosion of power went off inside her, blowing up disease and setting ablaze life and wholeness. This word *dynamis* is defined as strength power, miracle working power, influence, resources, and power consisting in armies.

This definitely sounds explosive to me. It is amazing that in a whole crowd, only one individual sought the source of such life-answering power for healing. While it seems that she was the victim of circumstances, further reflection points her out to be a victor by association.

This same word, "dynamis," is used by Christ while speaking to His disciples just before His ascension: "But you will receive *power*" (Acts 1:8). How would they receive this power? "When the Holy Spirit comes on you" (Acts 1:8). The very same explosive, life-giving power of God is readily available for every woman of God. We have access to His Spirit right in our own hearts. If we haven't tapped into His dynamite power, it's like having a gold bar buried in our backyard, while we're begging for money! Once we find out how to get the gold, we would do all we needed to dig the hole and benefit from the hole's content.

Well, my sister, call yourself lucky, because we just struck it rich—in the Holy Spirit, that is! This unnamed woman has given us the secret to find the gold of God's dynamis in our lives: If we just refuse to give up and do our part, we win.

I pray the Lord grant that we seek Him and receive His explosive life flowing in our situation, just as she did that day.

Faith Confessions

WE HAVE REASON TO HOPE WHEN OTHERS DO NOT UNDERSTAND

I will hope even when
there is no hope to have.
Romans 4:18

I will walk by faith and not by sight.
2 Corinthians 5:7

I will hope for what I cannot see
and with patience wait for it.
Romans 8:25

I will have faith
(the substance of things hoped for,
the evidence of things not seen).
Hebrews 11:1

I live by faith and I will not give up.
God has pleasure in me.
Hebrews 10:38

Life Principle 9

God Sees Me

Mark 5:32
But Jesus kept looking around to
see who had done it.

Everyone began to look among the members of the crowd. "Who touched Jesus?" Others shrugged their shoulders at the lack of finding this "guilty" person. Jesus turned and saw her. Her eyes met with His in a fearful glance. She was still gripping the seam of her dress, ready to run from the scene. She knew she was caught.

I believe He saw more than her tattered clothes and tear-stained eyes. He saw into her soul. He saw all her pain. Consider the woman in this text. She had been labeled an outcast because of her condition. It was against the law for her to be in public, let alone to touch anyone (Lev. 15). She must have been wounded both physically and emotionally. He saw her years of suffering. He saw her heart's desire to be whole. And when He saw her, He had compassion for her.

The woman's plan to slip back through the crowd and leave unnoticed was interrupted. She was not trying to make a scene. All she wanted was to be healed. *No one was supposed to know.*

What would happen to her? Would she be banished from the community for touching another person? Would she be stoned to death? Suddenly, her life was flashing before her as she realized that Someone knew what she had done.

My Special Moments

Reflect on God's attribute of being all-knowing. Write down how you feel when you know you've been "caught" by God for the godly and ungodly things in life. The list can be as long or as short as you wish. After you write down your thoughts, take time to pray aloud to God.

_____

_____

_____

_____

_____

_____

_____

_____

_____

_____

_____

_____

_____

_____

_____

_____

Prayer

Dear Father, there is no place I can hide from You. When I do what is right you see me. When I do what is wrong, You see me. You care for me at all times. You look at me and see into my heart. You know what I have done, but You also know *why*. Thank You for knowing all about me (pray about the thoughts you wrote down). In Jesus' Name, I know that You understand me. Amen.

Going Deeper

He saw her. I just love that. It means so much to me to know that God sees me. That means He's paying attention.

There have been times I've longed for my husband to see me. I would wait for him to comment on my hair or compliment my outfit. But he would walk past and... nothing. I would wonder, *Did he notice I got my hair cut or that I have on a new dress?* And then there are times he does notice me, and I'm not even trying to get his attention. He may compliment my makeup or crawl close to me in the bed. I really enjoy those moments. I feel most loved when I know he *sees* me.

How about if a boss would just *see* me? I deserve that promotion at work, because I worked hard on that project. What if my mom would *see* me? She would know I was hurting even though I was smiling and find out what's wrong. I wonder sometimes if my kids *see* me. Do they notice the sacrifices I make so that they don't have to go without? Wouldn't it be nice if people would really *see* me?

He saw her.

Eido means to see and perceive with the eyes and includes turning the mind's attention to and ascertaining what must be done about a state or condition. A minister once explained our relationship with Christ as one of intimacy, using the phrase, "Into me see."

This intimacy with Christ is the equivalent of being spiritually naked and still being held. There is no greater feeling of acceptance than to be fully known and still desired.

There is no other place to experience this type of intimacy. He saw her when no one else even cared to look upon her. He saw her at a point of accepting some messy realities about her. He saw her in a moment she thought was secret. In that kind of embarrassing nakedness, He saw her. And He would soon accept all that it meant.

Faith Confessions

GOD SEES ME

You knew me
and gave me purpose
since before my birth.
Jeremiah 1:5

I am fearfully and wonderfully made
because You created me
from my mother's womb.
Psalm 139: 13,14

Grace and peace are mine
because I am beloved of God.
Romans 1:7

It is not about *me*, but *me in Christ*.
I am receiving from God
wisdom, righteousness,
sanctification, and redemption.
1 Corinthians 1: 30

Blessings are not based upon me.
They are free gifts of grace.
By grace He accepts me.
Romans 5:15–18

Life Principle 10

Someone Needs to Hear My Testimony

Mark 5:33
... came and fell at his feet and,
trembling with fear, told him the
whole truth.

When she discovered that Jesus knew who she was, she could not resist Him. She came before Him and fell at His feet. The pace of her heartbeat grew faster and faster as she drew near, yet still she came.

Once again, the crowd was silenced. They stood by as she told of how she had been ill with the flow of blood for twelve years. They listened intently to her retell the horror of going from doctor to doctor, only to be sent home with a worse condition. She told them how, when she had spent all her money and had nothing left to hope in, she had heard that Jesus was in town. She knew that He was the answer. He had to be.

She did not intend to make a scene, but there were so many people. She had known there would be consequences if she were caught touching Him. All she wanted was to be free. She only meant to touch His hem and then leave. However, at the moment she touched His garment, the power that went into her body surprised her. It all happened so fast. Instantly, she knew that her blood had dried up, but she was afraid to say anything. And when she heard Him ask, "Who touched Me?" she feared that she would be discovered. Before she could run, she saw Him looking at her from the distance and knew that she was caught.

Think of who was in the crowd that day as she forced the words through her trembling lips. All of them heard her testimony. Consider the thoughts of those present. Some may have doubted. Others may have just stood by in awe. But surely some became believers. Remember who was there: the disciples and Jairus. They must have needed her testimony.

My Special Moments

Reflect on a time when overhearing someone else's testimony blessed you. Jot down how you feel about God's ability to turn painful situations around and then use them to help others. The list can be as long or as short as you wish. After you write down your thoughts, take time to pray aloud to God.

_____

_____

_____

_____

_____

_____

_____

_____

_____

_____

_____

_____

_____

Prayer

Dear Father, You know how to turn around bad situations. When a situation seems to be unbearable, You still find a way to bring glory out of it. Thank You for encouraging me through someone else's testimony (pray about the thoughts you wrote down). In Jesus' Name, I ask that You would use the testimonies of my life to help others. Amen.

Going Deeper

She fell down at His feet (*prospipto*). She came and showed humility and honor to Him before the crowd. Unsure of what others might think and knowing she had every reason to run away, she came trembling back and prostrated herself at His feet. The word for "fear," *phobeo,* means that she was struck with fear, but it also entails reverential obedience. I believe at the very moment of anxious fear she also displayed this reverential fear of Christ.

It's funny how time can go by so slowly and so quickly at the same time. I was at a wedding reception, and it was time for the father of the bride to speak. He made a comment along the lines of remembering when she was just a baby, and it seemed like he just blinked his eyes and she was getting married. At that moment, all those twenty years of her life felt like a blink.

I believe these very few seconds or minutes for the woman must have felt like an eternity to her. The twelve years of suffering had come to a very abrupt halt in that frozen moment. Everyone was looking at her. They would know she wasn't supposed to be there.

Despite the impending repercussions of her social disgrace, she declared to Him and to the crowd her complete story. In that instance, as she lay at the feet of Jesus, her life stood taller than them all. Not everything that brings us to our lowest point degrades us. He can take those low points and lift us above the crowds.

Faith Confessions

SOMEONE NEEDS TO HEAR MY TESTIMONY

I learn from the life of others
and others learn from my life.
Romans 15:4

My life is a living testimony
of the work of God.
2 Corinthians 3:2

I will say of the Lord
He is my refuge and I trust Him.
Psalm 91:2

I will let the light of God
shine in my life for others to see.
Matthew 5:16

As God restores me
and upholds me,
I will be able to help others seek Him.
Psalm 51:12, 13

Life Principle 11

God Wants a Relationship with Me

Mark 5:34
He said to her, "Daughter ..."

The first word out of His mouth was "Daughter." Jesus acknowledged a relationship with her. She was a daughter of God, and He was her Savior. She must have been startled by this response. She had assumed she would be punished, but she found mercy in the place of judgment.

Her faith made her well. It was not the fact that she had faith, but the object of her faith was the cause of her healing. Her faith in the doctors failed her. Her faith in the money failed her. Her faith in Jesus *saved* her.

Jesus gave her two directions. First, she was to go in peace. She had come to Him in turmoil. She had been sick and tired of being sick and tired. Second, she was to be healed of her affliction. The healing in her body was hers for the keeping. She would not have to be concerned about the hemorrhage tormenting her body any longer. There would be no return of the ailment or its symptoms.

She was finally free, and Jesus proclaimed it. All the people standing near must have been amazed at His response. He spoke gently with this woman. He had no intention of accusing her of any wrong. He supported her actions and comforted her with His words. He had claimed her as one of His own.

My Special Moments

Reflect on your relationship with God. Write down how you feel about being a "daughter" of the Most High. The list can be as long or as short as you wish. After you write down your thoughts, take time to pray aloud to God.

_____

_____

_____

_____

_____

_____

_____

_____

_____

_____

_____

_____

_____

_____

Prayer

Dear Father, I am Your child. I benefit in my life by my relationship to You. You make a difference in my life and cause me to be blessed by my connection with You. Thank You for caring for me as your very own (pray about the thoughts you wrote down). In Jesus' Name, I am happy to have a Father like You. Amen.

Going Deeper

Of all the names she had ever been called, "daughter" was the most honorable. After years of being socially outcast, the most important person in the crowd bestowed a title of kindness and even more intimately, kinship. *Thygatēr* means a daughter of God, who is acceptable to God, and one who rejoices in God's distinctive care and protection.

When He called her *Thygatēr* for daughter, she didn't just hear a word of family relation; she knew what it *meant*. And so did the crowd. They all knew that although she wasn't supposed to be there, she was now welcome in their presence. She was *accepted* for who she was and what she had from what she had come. She also knew it meant that she could finally rejoice. She probably hadn't done much rejoicing in the past few years. I'm sure this came as refreshing news! She would now experience a new season of care and protection.

He stopped for her because, as Jairus cared so deeply for his daughter, so the Heavenly Father cared for her. This interruption in Jairus's walk should have encouraged him, proving Jesus understood a father's heart for a daughter. It is the exact word of endearment that Jairus used in reference to his own child (Mark 5:23).

Faith Confessions

GOD WANTS A RELATIONSHIP WITH ME

I am a child of God
and He is my father.
Romans 8:15; Galatians 4:6

I communicate with God as my Father.
Matthew 6:6

I have access to the benefits
of God's fatherhood in my life.
Ephesians 2:18

Because I believe God,
like Abraham, God considers me
His friend.
James 2:23

God is mindful of me and visits me.
Psalm 8:4

Life Principle 12

Only God Has the Saving Power I Need

Matthew 9:22
And the woman was healed
from that moment.

No more blood flow. No more tears. No more pain. No more rejection. The woman the Son set free was free indeed (John 8:36). All her burdens and discouragement were washed away in that moment. She came in contact with a Living Jesus, who gave her a living hope, and she left with a living testimony.

The members of the crowd were once again astounded by this Man. They whispered among themselves. "Who is this Man from Nazareth?" "Who is this Man that heals?" "Is He a prophet?" "Is He Elijah?" They may not have come to a conclusion that day, but they left with faith in their hearts that He was more than a Man.

How about the disciples? They had been with Jesus. The disciples were there when He taught on the mountain (Mt. 5–7). Peter witnessed the healing of his own mother-in-law (Mt. 8). When they were afraid on the stormy seas, He calmed the winds and the waves (Luke 8). He ate with sinners (Mark 2) and accepted those who were unschooled to be His disciples. And yet, they were unable to discern His ability to be touched by the heart of this woman.

Jairus must have been encouraged. Even if he was disappointed in the delay of getting to his own sick daughter, he had to have felt some comfort in witnessing firsthand Jesus heal this woman. Jesus was no longer just Someone who Jairus heard of. Now Jesus was Someone with whom Jairus had come into contact. Jesus was exactly who Jairus had hoped He would be. He was the son of man and the Son of God (Mark 15:39): Jesus the Christ.

My Special Moments

Reflect on God's deity. Jot down how you feel about God being more powerful than man, more powerful than the devil, more powerful than life's situations. The list can be as long or as short as you wish. After you write down your thoughts, take time to pray aloud to God.

_____

_____

_____

_____

_____

_____

_____

_____

_____

_____

_____

_____

_____

Prayer

Dear Father, You are the Great I am. You alone are more than enough. You are my salvation from whatever I need saving. Thank You for being my hope beyond hope (pray about the thoughts you wrote down). In Jesus' Name, I worship You. You are the reason I have found my moment to be healed. Amen.

Going Deeper

"From that moment": *hōra,* a certain definite time or point in time. There was a destined point in time for her to find this moment in her life. Perhaps she held fast to the principal Habakkuk teaches us: "For the vision [is] yet for an appointed time, but at the end it shall speak, and not lie: though it tarry, wait for it; because it will surely come, it will not tarry" (Hab. 2:3).

How did she find her moment? She found it because she would not give up; therefore, the moment surely came. In all of the lessons we learn from watching this crowd, the biggest lesson of all is that of God's faithfulness to those who refuse to stop asking, seeking, and knocking (Mt. 7:7). I leave you with these words from Luke 18 NIV,

> [1]Then Jesus told his disciples a parable to show them that they should always pray and not give up. [2]He said: "In a certain town there was a judge who neither feared God nor cared what people thought. [3]And there was a widow in that town who kept coming to him with the plea, 'Grant me justice against my adversary.' [4]"For some time he refused. But finally he said to himself, 'Even though I don't fear God or care what people think, [5]yet because this widow keeps bothering me, I will see that she gets justice, so that she won't eventually come and attack me!'" [6]And the

Lord said, "Listen to what the unjust judge says. ⁷And will not God bring about justice for his chosen ones, who cry out to him day and night? Will he keep putting them off? ⁸I tell you, he will see that they get justice, and quickly. However, when the Son of Man comes, will he find faith on the earth?"

Faith Confessions

Only God Has the Saving Power I Need

God is a very present help to me
in troubled times of life.
Psalm 46:1

I am more than a conqueror
because God loves me.
Romans 8:37

Jesus' cross disarmed the enemy
and triumphed on my behalf.
Colossians 2:15

In God is my salvation.
Psalm 62:7

I put on daily the whole armor of God.
Ephesians 6:13–18

A Prayer for Salvation

Dear Lord, I know that I am a sinner. I have made mistakes and desire for You to help me. I want to be right with You. I know Jesus is the Son of God. I believe He died for all my sins. I believe He rose from the grave and will come again. Help me to understand my Salvation. Guide me to a church family to love me and for me to love in return. Help me to know what my gifts are and give me opportunities to glorify You. Deliver me from my past life and help me to know You make all things new. I want to be continually filled with Your Holy Spirit. Teach me how to live each day for You. Thank You for saving me. Amen

About the Author

Lisa Davis has formally served in church ministry work since 2009 but has been involved with speaking and Bible teaching for much longer. She held her first women's conference, Diamonds in the Rough, in December 2008, encouraging women to move "From Soot to Shine." Prior to this, Lisa taught adult Sunday school as well as worked alongside others in teaching youth church services. Lisa has been a frequent Bible teacher for Midweek Bible study and has been a requested speaker for prayer breakfast worship and women's retreats. Her current profession is in education, in which she has served families in both public and private school settings for over eleven years. She resides in Texas with her husband, Michael, and their two daughters. Lisa can be contacted for testimonies, prayer support, or speaking inquires by e-mail at LisaDavis@ everylady.org.

Bibliography

Blue Letter Bible. http://www.blueletterbible.org/index. cfm. Hebrew-Greek Lexicon.

Ressler, A. J. *Under His Wings* http://www.therefinersfire. org/tallit.htm. 21 March 2006.

Vine, W. E. *Vine's Expository Dictionary of Old & New Testament Words.* Nashville, TN: Thomas Nelson, 1997.

Printed in the United States
by Baker & Taylor Publisher Services